Guard Dogs

By Mary Ann Hoffman

Gareth Stevens
Publishing

Please visit our Web site, www.garethstevens.com. For a free color catalog of all our high-quality books, call toll free 1-800-542-2595 or fax 1-877-542-2596.

Library of Congress Cataloging-in-Publication Data

Hoffman, Mary Ann, 1947-
Guard dogs / Mary Ann Hoffman.
   p. cm.
Includes index.
ISBN 978-1-4339-4648-6 (pbk.)
ISBN 978-1-4339-4649-3 (6-pack)
ISBN 978-1-4339-4647-9 (library binding)
1. Watchdogs—Juvenile literature. I. Title.
SF428.8.H64 2011
636.73—dc22

                           2010035241

First Edition

Published in 2011 by
Gareth Stevens Publishing
111 East 14th Street, Suite 349
New York, NY 10003

Copyright © 2011 Gareth Stevens Publishing

Designer: Michael J. Flynn
Editor: Kristen Rajczak

Photo credits: Cover, pp. 1, 9, 10, 13, 17, 18, 20 Shutterstock.com; pp. 5, 6, 14 iStockphoto.com.

Printed in the United States of America

CPSIA compliance information: Batch #CW11GS: For further information contact Gareth Stevens, New York, New York at 1-800-542-2595.

Contents

Words in the glossary appear in **bold** type the first time they are used in the text.

What Is a Guard Dog?

A guard dog is a dog used to watch and **protect** people and property. Guard dogs are smart and strong. Sometimes they might look a little scary. Guard dogs bark to let their owners know when something doesn't seem right or when they sense danger. Guard dogs attack unwelcome people and animals to keep them from causing harm. They're trained to obey commands. Guard dogs are used for family protection, **security**, and keeping other animals safe.

Dog Tales

Some people believe that female dogs are best at protecting people. They think male dogs are best at protecting property.

A guard dog is part of the family it protects.

Dog Tales

A watchdog is different from a guard dog. Watchdogs usually just bark a warning but don't become forceful.

The children in this family have fun with and take good care of their guard dog. ▷

6

Guarding Homes and Families

Guard dogs keep families and their homes safe. They're **loyal**, loving, friendly, and gentle. Guard dogs warn their owners when something isn't right. Then, they follow their owner's commands. Home and family guard dogs start training as puppies to get along with people and other animals. They become forceful only when they sense danger or are given a sign by their owner.

Security

Companies use guard dogs to keep areas safe and secure. Most security guard dogs live at the place they're guarding. Security guard dogs receive different training than home and family guard dogs do. Guard dogs are chosen because it's in their **nature** to guard and protect. These features are strengthened in security guard dogs. They're trained to prevent unwanted people and animals from entering an area. They usually act on their own without needing a command.

Dog Tales

Some security guard dogs don't work on their own. They work with their trainers.

Doberman pinschers are loyal security dogs.

Dog Tales

A livestock guard dog meets the animals it will guard while it is still a puppy. It grows up with these animals as its "family."

A good livestock guard dog is protective, watchful, and dependable.

Protecting Other Animals

Some guard dogs protect other animals. Because they're watchful and quick, they can keep groups of animals safe from **predators**. These guard dogs are usually large. They don't control the movements of the animals they're guarding. Instead, they mix in with the animals while watching for danger. Depending on the number of animals being guarded, several livestock guard dogs may work together.

Doberman Pinschers

Many **breeds** can be trained as guard dogs. Let's look at some of the more common breeds used.

Doberman pinschers make excellent guard dogs. They're smart, watchful, and loyal dogs. Dobermans are easy to recognize. They're commonly black with brown on their faces and feet. They're **muscular** and have very short hair. Dobermans are fast, have a lot of spirit, and are quick thinking. They can easily be trained to obey. Dobermans can be forceful toward strangers, so proper training is very important.

Dog Tales

The Doberman pinscher was named after the man who began the breed, Karl Dobermann.

Doberman pinschers usually have **cropped** ears to help them hear better.

Dog Tales

Boxers like to stand on their back legs and use their front paws to hit at things.

Boxers like attention and love from their owners! ▷

14

Boxers

Boxers are medium-sized dogs with strong legs, short hair, and a broad face. Their heads have a square shape when viewed from the side. Boxers are brown or brown with other colors mixed in. They're loyal, hardworking, and playful. Boxers are wonderful dogs for a family because they like a lot of activity but are gentle, loving, and protective. They're quick learners and can be easily trained to watch over both people and property.

American Bulldogs

American bulldogs are medium-sized to large dogs with muscular bodies and very strong **jaws**. American bulldogs are usually white with brown spots. They're very powerful and active. They're curious, fearless, and aware of the people and things around them. American bulldogs are dependable and not overly forceful. They get along well with other dogs and people. American bulldogs are easily trained to follow commands and are quick to obey.

Dog Tales

American bulldogs have a strong protective **instinct**.

There are two basic kinds of American bulldogs—Johnson and Scott.

17

Dog Tales

Bullmastiffs were raised in England to chase and hold down people who hunted animals on other people's land. The dogs were trained to do this without causing harm.

Bullmastiffs tend to slobber and drool, especially after eating.

Bullmastiffs

A bullmastiff is a large, powerful dog with a great sense of smell. Bullmastiffs move quietly and are unafraid. They're light brown, red, or a mix of brown and other colors. Bullmastiffs are known as brave protectors of people and property. They're smart, loyal, and want to please their owners. Bullmastiffs are usually quiet and don't bark a lot. Because of their size and the way they look, they can be very scary to strangers.

Many Jobs

Many breeds of dogs are trained as guard dogs to do many different jobs. They warn people of danger and protect them from harm. They watch and protect property. They keep other animals safe. Would you like to have one of the guard dogs you've just read about?

Guard Dog Sizes

	Height	Weight
Doberman pinscher	24–28 inches (61–71 cm)	66–88 pounds (30–40 kg)
boxer	21–25 inches (53–64 cm)	55–70 pounds (25–32 kg)
American bulldog	22–28 inches (56–71 cm)	70–120 pounds (32–54 kg)
bullmastiff	24–27 inches (61–69 cm)	100–120 pounds (45–54 kg)

Glossary

breed: a group of animals that share features different from other groups of the kind

crop: to cut off part of the outside of the ear so that it stands up

instinct: a natural ability

jaws: the upper and lower parts of the mouth

loyal: faithful

muscular: having powerful, strong muscles

nature: character

predator: an animal that kills and eats other animals

protect: to keep safe

security: safety

For More Information

Books:

Green, Sara. *Boxers*. Minneapolis, MN: Bellwether Media, 2009.

Stone, Lynn M. *Bulldogs*. Vero Beach, FL: Rourke Publishing, 2007.

Urbigkit, Cat. *Brave Dogs, Gentle Dogs: How They Guard Sheep*. Honesdale, PA: Boyds Mills Press, 2005.

Web Sites:

American Kennel Club: Kids' Corner

www.akc.org/public_education/kids_corner/kidscorner.cfm

Read an online newsletter and do activities about responsible dog ownership.

Good Guard Dogs

www.gopetsamerica.com/dogs/guard-dogs.aspx

Learn about guard dogs. Read facts and view pictures of popular breeds.

Index